# Footprints on the Roof

poems about the earth

by Marilyn Singer

illustrated by Meilo So

Alfred A. Knopf
New York

For
Walter Mayes
and Valerie Lewis

THIS IS A BORZOI BOOK PUBLISHED BY ALFRED A. KNOPF

Text copyright © 2002 by Marilyn Singer
Illustrations copyright © 2002 by Meilo So

www.randomhouse.com/kids

*Library of Congress Cataloging-in-Publication Data*
Singer, Marilyn
Footprints on the roof : poems about the earth / by Marilyn Singer ;
illustrated by Meilo So.
p. cm.
ISBN 0-375-81094-3 (trade) − ISBN 0-375-91094-8 (lib. bdg.)
1. Earth−Juvenile poetry. 2. Children's poetry, American.
[1. Nature−Poetry. 2. Earth−Poetry. 3. American poetry.] I. So, Meilo, ill.
II. Title.
PS3569.I546 F66 2002
811'.54−dc21     2001029407

Printed in the United States of America

February 2002

10   9   8   7   6   5   4   3   2   1

First Edition

# Contents

# Home

Ask me where is home
and I will tell you
a house
a street
a neighborhood
a town
Someplace safe and solid
where I eat
I run
I sing
I nap
Someplace I can pinpoint
on a map
But what if I were an astronaut
with the world dangling below me
like a yo-yo from a giant's hand
and home was the whole planet?
Would I be wise enough to understand
the worth
of my new address:      Earth

## Burrows

Out in the country I walk across towns
    I'll never see:
mazy metropolises
    under the earth
        where rabbits hide from foxes
          foxes hide from dogs
          full-bellied snakes sleep snugly
            worms work uncomplaining

Where what you see is nothing—
what counts is what you smell
            or hear or feel
I try to tread softly:
      a quiet giant
                  leaving only footprints
                        on the roof

## Dining Out

Each day I eat the earth
        I drink the rain
They taste celery-bitter
              watermelon-sweet
Their flavor
          subtle
              bold
    is stored
in every grain of rice
      in every stalk of wheat
in every root
      leaf
      shoot
harvested in Chile
    or in China
        or at Fanelli's farm
Each day I eat the earth
      I drink the rain
And my tongue
             is never bored

## Go-Betweens

Trees are go-betweens
    listening to the stories
of both earth and sky
      the conversations
of vireos and star-nosed moles
    of eagles and worms
Trees know the soft secrets of clouds
    the dark siftings of soil
They hear the high keening of squalls
      the deep rumbling of rocks
Trees whisper for the sky's damp blessings
    and the earth's misty kisses
They issue warnings
They offer praise
    This is trees' work
and they do it with such uncomplaining grace
    it never seems like work at all

## Summer Solstice

Amid the scent of roses
    and the lulling hum of bees
comes a cloud scudding briefly across the sun
    or a slightly pointed breeze
to remind you that the earth has turned again
    and in a long slow wink
        the nights will grow
        the days will shrink
The richest garden
    the greenest trees
will have a different form
    wearing withered leaves like memories
        of days when it was warm

## Natural Disasters

We were talking disasters
      scaring ourselves
          with what on earth would scare us:
Volcanoes venting red-hot rivers
           spumes of ash
      like barbecues gone crazy
Earthquakes that crack the world
      like a walnut
Sandstorms that suffocate
Tidal waves that drown
      Hurricanes, tornadoes
       avalanches, floods
And blizzards
      simple blizzards—
those frightened me the most
      trapping me right there in my house
        with nothing to eat
      but my shoes

We were talking disasters

feeling the earth go wobbly

leaving ourselves

with no place to hide

Until right outside my window

a robin chirruped loudly

in the hickory tree

like nothing on earth mattered

but its song

And suddenly the room righted itself

the floor held steady

and we knew that we were safe

for at least another day

## Dormant Dragons

Volcanoes there are that sleep
　　　　the sleep of dragons
With cool heads and hot bellies
　　　　they crouch
　　　　　　　solid and still
　　　　where the earth meets the sky
Till something wakes them
　　　　Then furious they breathe fire and smoke
　　　　　　　　　　hot spittle and wrath
　　　　　to burn and choke
　　　　　　　whatever lies in their path
　　　　leaving in their wake
　　　　　　　an odd treasure
　　of stone sponges and glass
　　　　　　　and an occasional lake

# Caves

The thing about caves
       is you go so deep
             inside the earth
       you think that you have left it
Stalactites
       Stalagmites
Rivers made of crystal
       Flowers made of stone
Untraveled landscapes
       sunless
            moonless
from maybe some other galaxy
       where bats and beetles rule
and there are twenty words for darkness
       but none at all
                     for light

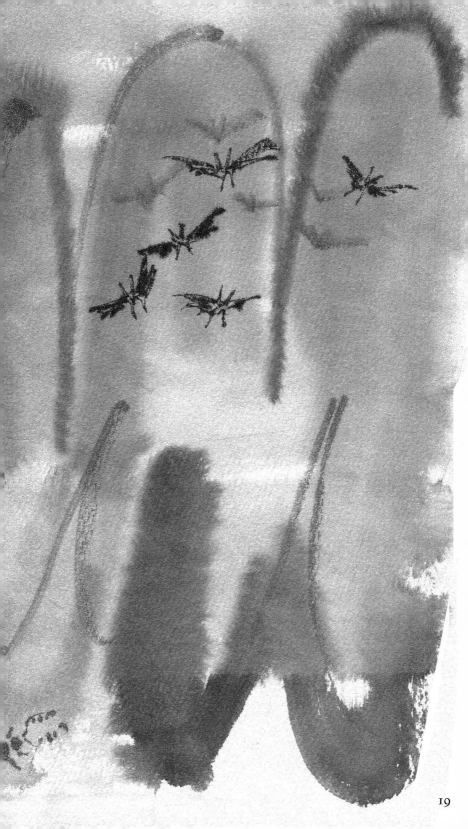

## Prehistoric Praise

Dinosaurs get all the press
In books and movies
    on subway walls
        long-necked sauropods
        horn-headed triceratops
        sail-backs
            duck-bills
        and, yes indeed, terror-toothed Tyrannosaurus rex
            reign
Their big bones fill museum halls
Thrashing tail to gaping jaw
        they always inspire awe
But before
    way before reptiles ruled
    other creatures were here:
        sea scorpions the size of automobiles
        dragonflies the size of kites
        fish that climbed to shore
            on finny feet
        trilobites with twenty thousand eyes
        ancestral sharks and gliding rays
They left their shells
    their shape
    their ambition
  on the Earth
They too have worth
    They also amaze

## Back to Nature

We cover the earth
    with asphalt
        tarmac
        concrete
        brick
We want to be far away
    from humus
        moss and leaf mold
    from things soft and unpredictable
        that slide beneath our feet
But even in the city
    sparrows nest in lampposts
        tree trunks rise from sewers
    and mulberries fat and purple
        rain on sidewalks
    turning the pavement soft and unpredictable
        making it slide beneath our feet

# Mud

Sometimes I'm in the mood
                    for mud
When my toes have tasted
            too many sidewalks
When my knees have stayed
            too clean
            too unused
When the earth is
            a cake without frosting
            or a sundae without sauce
Then I cheer on rain and thunder
            and forget about my shoes
In the park
            or by the river
I choose
                            ooze

## Winter Solstice

On December twenty-first
    shiny
        black-booted
    warmly snow-suited
I pick and lick an icicle
    and pretend I'm in Australia
where it is the first morning of summer
        on the other side of the earth
And I know that someone there
    sandy
        bare-footed
    coolly bathing-suited
will buy and try an ice cream cone
    and pretend she's in America
where it is the first morning of winter
    on the other side of the earth

# Ice

The same night the window cracked
        the rain turned hard-hearted
        the ground turned mean
and we woke to a world of ice
Out on the street
        Dad windmilled like a slapstick dancer
        Mom crept like a mincing crab
We tried to tell them
        ice respects no one
If you can't lick it
        trick it
But they didn't want to hear
Then we looped our scarves across our faces
        so they couldn't see us laugh
and slid across the sidewalk
        like the earth was one big rink

## Islands

Dad likes to talk
     about islands—
how they sink
how they rise
How some are bred
     by volcanoes
and others built from coral bones
How some are crowned by castles
and some stripped clean
     even of trees
It's the earth playing peek-a-boo
     with the sea, he says
But to me it sounds
     a more dangerous game
And I think once in a while the sea
     just finds it amusing
          to let the earth
             win

## Fens

I'm a fan of fens
>of bogs, marshes and bayous—

those in-between places of the earth
>not quite water, not quite land

those untrustworthy places
>that make you watch where you stand

those horror movie places
>damp and thick with fog

full of jaws and flashing claws,
>scales and thrashing tails

You can't be bored in a bayou
>a fen, a marsh, a bog—

those misunderstood places
>where logs can have teeth
>>reeds can have wings

where the air so still, so quiet

always growls, buzzes, sings

# Desert

I want to be there when the desert blooms
To see hot pink and shining gold
      interrupt the endless tan
To dance among the cactuses
      sporting flowers in their spiky hair
To celebrate the birth of tadpoles
      swimming in sudden pools

I want to be there when the desert blooms
To watch this serious span of earth
      grow festive for a day
To revel in rain as something
      sacred and rare
To honor this peculiar place
      where hope is not for fools

# Dunes

There are dunes
> and there are dunes
Standing on the earth
> flat-footed and thirsty
we see only relentless sand
But from up high
> we gaze with pleasure
>> at ripples and ridges
>> crescents and spheres—
every dune a signature
> announcing its creator
each one a sculpture
> in a worldwide work of art

# Patience

I thought I would be taller
    in the mountains
A queen of green and brown
    my realm laid out below me
        neat as the rug Grandma hooked
    one St. Patrick's Day

I thought I would be braver
    in the mountains
Following the fierce paths
    of pumas and grizzlies
Ledge leaper
    Crag climber
Taking nothing for granted
    Leaving nothing unexplored

I thought I would be wiser
    in the mountains
Reading the history of the world
    in the weathered rocks
Hearing lectures
    in the wind and waterfalls
Stretching my mind
    broader than Grandpa's tall stories
        multiplied by ten

I thought I would be taller

braver

wiser

in the mountains

And I wasn't

But I am more patient

in the mountains

And I can wait

## Early Explorers

No place on earth
    is ever undiscovered
Even in Antarctica
    where whole mountains are hidden
        under ice
penguins already laid shambling tracks
      in the snow
    before we traveled there
The hottest desert
      the deepest jungle
    where none of us have ever been
all have been crossed
      and crossed again
    by wings whirring or silent
      feet furred or scaled
        hoofed or bare
By adventurers we will never know
    explorers who will never tell us
      what wonders they have seen